My World of Geography
DESERTS

Angela Royston

Heinemann Library
Chicago, Illinois

Customer Service 888-454-2279
Visit our website at www.heinemannlibrary.com

Design: Ron Kamen and Celia Jones
Illustrations: Barry Atkinson (p. 12), Jo Brooker (p. 15),
  Jeff Edwards (pp. 7, 28–29)
Photo Research: Rebecca Sodergren, Melissa Allison, and
  Debra Weatherley
Originated by Ambassador Litho
Printed and bound in China by South
 China Printing

09 08 07 06
10 9 8 7 6 5 4 3 2

**Library of Congress
Cataloging-in-Publication Data**

Royston, Angela.
   Deserts / Angela Royston.
      p. cm. – (My world of geography)
   Includes bibliographical references and index.
   ISBN 1-4034-5588-0 (HC), 1-4034-5597-X (Pbk)
   ISBN 978-1-4034-5588-8 (HC), 978-1-4034-5597-0 (Pbk)
   1. Deserts–Juvenile literature. I. Title. II. Series.
   GB612.R67 2005
   551.41'5–dc22

                              2004003849

Acknowledgments

The author and publisher are grateful to the following for
permission to reproduce copyright material:
pp. 4 (Photodisc), 5, 10 (Taxi), 11 (Photodisc) Getty
Images; pp. 6 (Goodshot), 14 (Barrie Rokeach), 18
(Lenscapp), 20 (Sylvain Grandadam) Alamy Images; p. 8
Nature Picture Library; pp. 9 (Steve Bein), 19 (Robert
Garvey), 26 (C. & J. Lenars) Corbis; pp. 13 (Giacomo
Pirozzi), 23, 27 (Clive Shirley) Panos Pictures; p. 16
Harcourt Education Ltd./Rob Bowden; p. 17 (Joseph
Robichaud Photography) Photographers Direct.com;
pp. 21, 22, 25 (Mark Edwards) Still Pictures; p. 24
(Dr. Jeremy Burgess) Science Photo Library.

Cover photograph reproduced with permission of Getty
Images/Image Bank.

Every effort has been made to contact copyright holders of
any material reproduced in this book. Any omissions will
be rectified in subsequent printings if notice is given to the
publisher.

Contents

Some words are shown in bold, **like this.** You can find out what they mean by looking in the glossary.

What Is a Desert?

A desert is an area of land that gets
very little rain. Most deserts are
in the hottest countries of the
world, but some deserts
are cold.

Deserts are so dry that very few plants can grow there. Some deserts are covered with sand. Others are covered mostly with stones and rocks.

Sandy Deserts

The Sahara is a desert region covered with sand. The sand forms hills called **dunes.** The dunes move as the wind blows the sand.

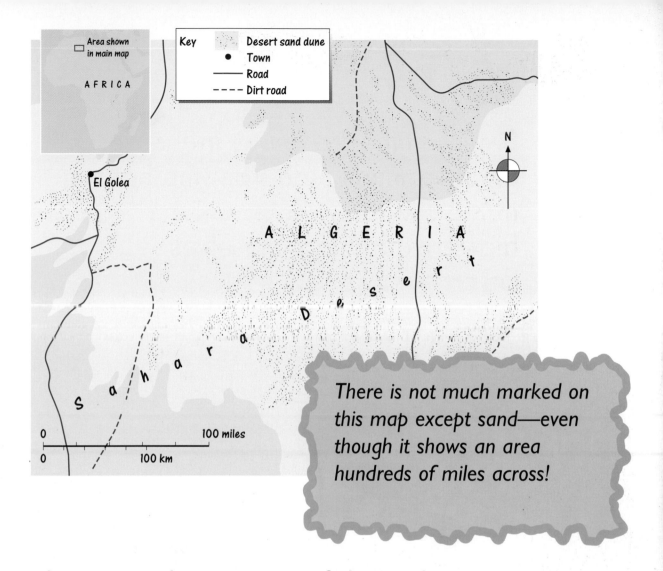

Area shown in main map

AFRICA

Key
Desert sand dune
● Town
— Road
--- Dirt road

El Golea

A L G E R I A

S a h a r a   D e s e r t

N

0   100 miles
0   100 km

There is not much marked on this map except sand—even though it shows an area hundreds of miles across!

This map shows part of the Sahara in Africa. It uses lots of black dots to show sand dunes and sandy desert. It shows only large areas of sand.

Desert Animals

Some animals can live in the desert. Small animals hide from the hot sun in the shade of rocks. Others hide by digging themselves **burrows.**

This kangaroo rat lives in the Arizona Desert.

These camels live in a desert in Mongolia.

Snakes, lizards, gerbils, and beetles are some of the animals that live in deserts. Most desert animals get the water they need from the food they eat.

Rainstorms

Sometimes it rains very hard in the desert. The rain soaks the ground and wildflowers grow quickly. For a few days, the desert is covered with flowers!

These wildflowers were photographed in a desert in Western Australia.

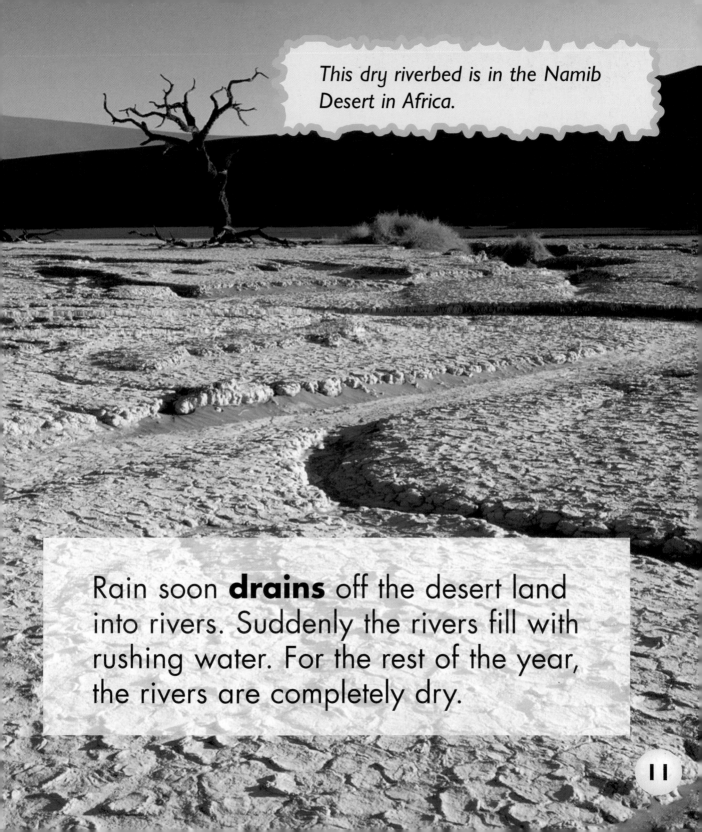

This dry riverbed is in the Namib Desert in Africa.

Rain soon **drains** off the desert land into rivers. Suddenly the rivers fill with rushing water. For the rest of the year, the rivers are completely dry.

An Oasis

An **oasis** is a place in the desert where there is water all year long. Usually the water in an oasis comes from an underground **pool** or river.

Rain falls on mountains and sinks through a layer of soft rock. The water gets trapped under deserts between layers of hard rock. People can reach it by digging wells.

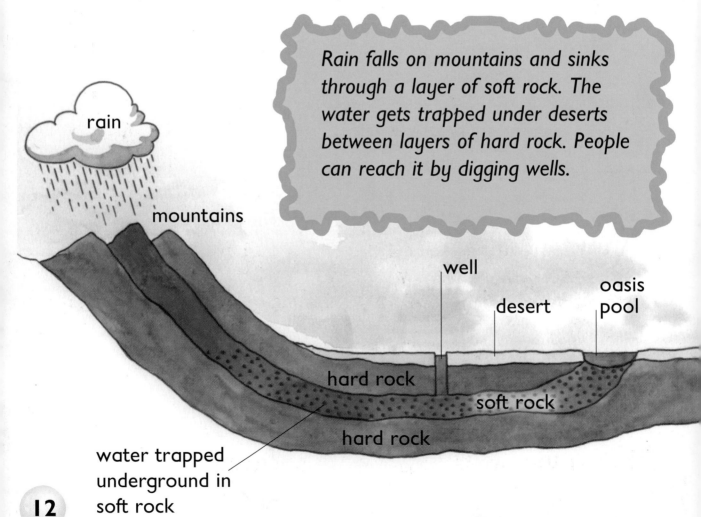

rain

mountains

well

desert

oasis pool

hard rock

soft rock

hard rock

water trapped underground in soft rock

This well in Egypt has a pump to bring water to the surface.

People dig deep **wells** to reach water under the desert ground. The wells have **pumps** or buckets to bring the water up to the surface.

Pools of Water

In some desert places, water bubbles to the surface and forms a **pool.** People may build a village around the **oasis** and grow **crops** there.

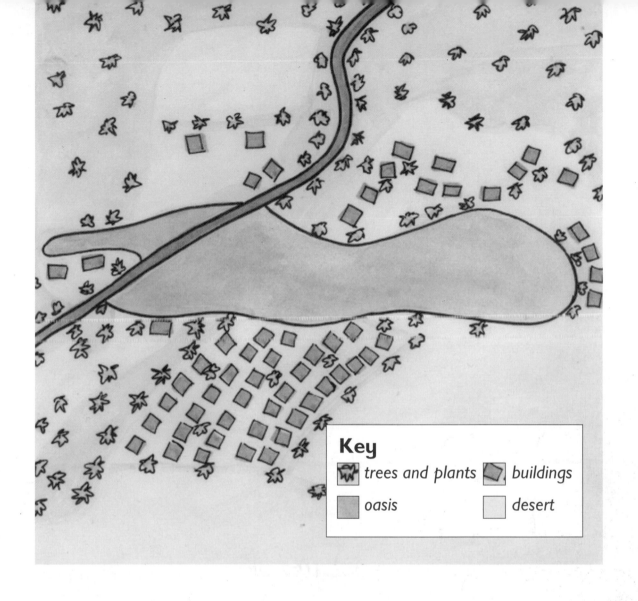

Key
trees and plants   buildings
oasis   desert

This map shows the same oasis as the photo on page 14. It shows the pool of water, the houses, the trees, and the desert beyond. You could draw a map like this.

Desert Towns and Cities

In Egypt, the Nile River flows through the Sahara. Many towns are built along the banks of the Nile River.

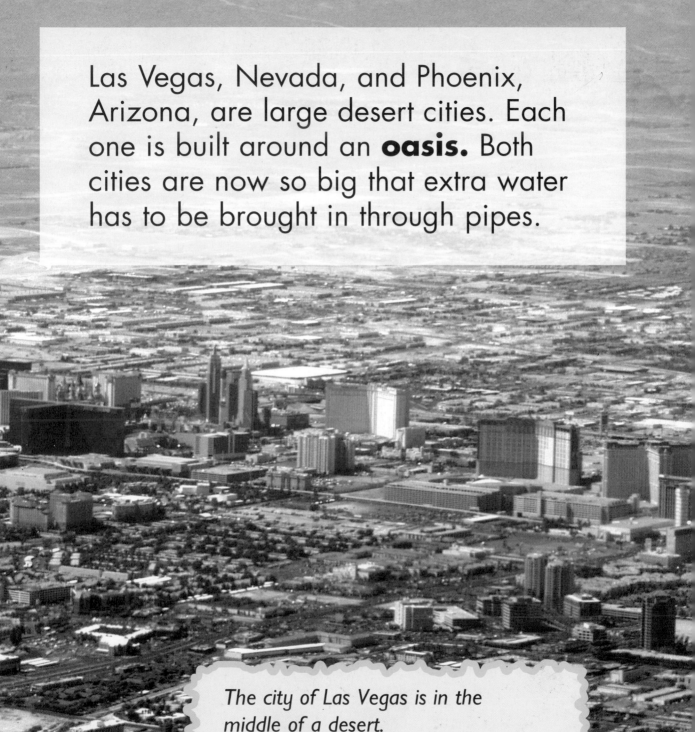

Las Vegas, Nevada, and Phoenix, Arizona, are large desert cities. Each one is built around an **oasis.** Both cities are now so big that extra water has to be brought in through pipes.

The city of Las Vegas is in the middle of a desert.

Mining the Desert

Many deserts have oil trapped far below the ground. Oil companies **drill** deep holes to reach the oil. The oil is then **pumped** to the surface.

*This oil **well** is in the Arabian Desert in Oman.*

This gold mine is in the middle of a desert in Australia.

Some deserts have **precious** stones and **metals** hidden in the rocky ground. In Australia, people **mine** diamonds, gold, and iron from the desert.

Crossing a Desert

It is easy to get lost in a desert because the roads often get covered up by sand. Visitors to the desert have to carry all the water they need with them.

In the Sahara, people often use camels to carry things across the desert. Camels store water in their stomachs. They can walk for many days without drinking water. Their humps are mounds of fat that help them survive without food.

Semidesert

Semidesert is land that is not quite as dry as a desert. The ground is dry and bare, but more plants grow there than in the desert itself.

*This **goatherd** in Yemen is looking after her goats.*

Many people live in semideserts. They often keep **cattle** or goats that feed on the few plants that grow there. They also plant **crops** in the dry earth.

Deserts Getting Bigger

Many semideserts are turning into deserts. This is because the world is becoming hotter and drier. Less rain means that **crops** do not grow well.

In some places, people are causing semideserts to turn into deserts. Their **cattle** and goats eat plants faster than the plants can grow again. People also cut down trees for **firewood.** Without trees to hold the soil in place, the wind blows it away.

Replanting Deserts

In some places, people are trying to stop their land from turning into desert. They plant **acacia** and other trees that grow quickly. **Cattle** can feed on these trees.

These people in the Sahara in Africa are planting a **windbreak** on a sand **dune.**

Some farmers use pipes to bring water for their **crops** from far away. They grow **cactuses** or other plants to shelter their crops from the wind.

Deserts of the World

This map shows where the largest deserts in the world are.
It also shows how big they are.

NORTH AMERICA

Great Basin Desert

Mojave Desert

Sonoran Desert

Chihuahuan Desert

SOUTH AMERICA

Atacama-Sechura Desert

Monte Desert

Patagonian Desert

North American Desert
Key fact: The North American Desert
is made up of several deserts
joined together.
Size: 478,000 sq miles
(1,240,000 sq km)

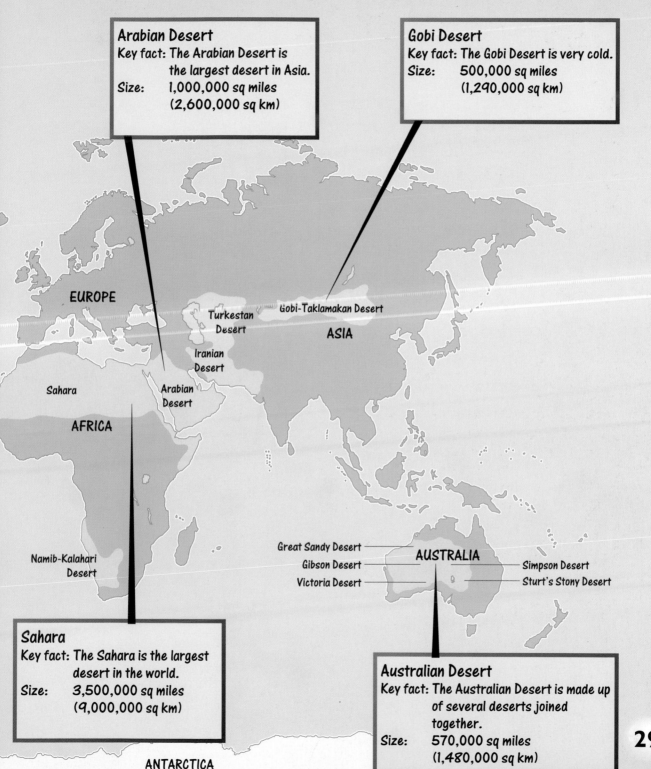

Arabian Desert
Key fact: The Arabian Desert is the largest desert in Asia.
Size: 1,000,000 sq miles (2,600,000 sq km)

Gobi Desert
Key fact: The Gobi Desert is very cold.
Size: 500,000 sq miles (1,290,000 sq km)

EUROPE

Turkestan Desert

Gobi-Taklamakan Desert

ASIA

Iranian Desert

Sahara

Arabian Desert

AFRICA

Namib-Kalahari Desert

Great Sandy Desert

AUSTRALIA

Gibson Desert

Simpson Desert

Victoria Desert

Sturt's Stony Desert

Sahara
Key fact: The Sahara is the largest desert in the world.
Size: 3,500,000 sq miles (9,000,000 sq km)

Australian Desert
Key fact: The Australian Desert is made up of several deserts joined together.
Size: 570,000 sq miles (1,480,000 sq km)

ANTARCTICA

Glossary

acacia kind of tree that grows fast in the desert

burrow underground hole that an animal digs

cactus type of plant with no leaves. Cactuses often grow in deserts because they do not need much water.

cattle cows, bulls, or oxen

crop plant grown for food

drains when water or other liquid flows from one place to another

drill make a hole by turning a long spike

dune hill of sand

firewood wood that is burned in a fire

goatherd someone who takes care of goats

metal hard, shiny material

mine dig a hole in the ground to get something valuable, such as metals or coal

oasis place in the desert where there is water

pool dip or hole in the ground that is filled with water

precious of great value or high price

pump use a machine to make water flow up or along a pipe

well hole dug in the ground to reach water or oil

windbreak something built to stop the wind from blowing things away

More Books to Read

Ashwell, Miranda, and Andy Owen. *Deserts.* Chicago: Heinemann Library, 1998.

Fowler, Allan. *Living in a Desert.* Danbury, Conn.: Scholastic Library, 2000.

Gaff, Jackie. *I Wonder Why the Sahara Is Cold at Night and Other Questions about Deserts.* Boston: Houghton Mifflin, 2004.

Galko, Francine. *Desert Animals.* Chicago: Heinemann Library, 2003.

Geisert, Bonnie, and Arthur Geisert. *Desert Town.* Boston: Houghton Mifflin, 2001.

Klingel, Cynthia Fitterer, and Robert B. Noyed. *Deserts.* Chanhassen, Minn.: Child's World, 2001.

Wilkins, Sally. *Deserts.* Mankato, Minn.: Capstone Press, 2001.

Index